A Note to Parents

DK READERS is a compelling program for beginning readers, designed in conjunction with leading literacy experts, including Dr. Linda Gambrell, Professor of Education at Clemson University. Dr. Gambrell has served as President of the National Reading Conference and the College Reading Association, and the International Reading Association.

Beautiful illustrations and superb full-color photographs combine with engaging, easy-to-read stories to offer a fresh approach to each subject in the series. Each DK READER is guaranteed to capture a child's interest while developing his or her reading skills, general knowledge, and love of reading.

The five levels of DK READERS are aimed at different reading abilities, enabling you to choose the books that are exactly right for your child:

Pre-level 1: Learning to read
Level 1: Beginning to read
Level 2: Beginning to read alone
Level 3: Reading alone
Level 4: Proficient readers

The "normal" age at which a child begins to read can be anywhere from three to eight years old. Adult participation through the lower levels is very helpful for providing encouragement, discussing storylines, and sounding out unfamiliar words.

No matter which level you select, you can be sure that you are helping your child learn to read, then read to learn!

LONDON, NEW YORK, MUNICH,
MELBOURNE, AND DELHI

Editorial Lead Heather Jones
DTP Designer David McDonald
Senior Production Controller Rachel Lloyd
Associate Publisher Nigel Duffield

Reading Consultant
Linda Gambrell, Ph.D.

Produced by
Shoreline Publishing Group LLC
President James Buckley, Jr.
Designer Tom Carling, carlingdesign.com

The Boy Scouts of America®, Cub Scouts®,
Boys' Life®, and rank insignia are registered
trademarks of the Boy Scouts of America.
Printed under license from the
Boy Scouts of America.

First American Edition, 2011
11 12 13 14 10 9 8 7 6 5 4 3 2 1
Published in the United States by DK Publishing
375 Hudson Street, New York, New York 10014

Published in Great Britain by Dorling Kindersley Limited

DK books are available at special discounts when purchased in bulk
for sales promotions, premiums, fund-raising, or educational use.
For details, contact:
DK Publishing Special Markets,
375 Hudson Street, New York, New York 10014
SpecialSales@dk.com

A catalog record for this book is available
from the Library of Congress.
ISBN: 978-0-7566-5038-4

Printed and bound in China by L. Rex Printing Company

The publisher would like to thank the following for their kind
permission to reproduce their photographs:
(Key: a=above; b=below/bottom; c=center; l=left; r=right; t=top)
Corbis: 16, 20, 28; Dreamstime.com (photographers listed): Melissa Dockstader 39t,
Fallsview 19, Steffan Foerster 23, Michael Madsen 19, Oleg Mitiukhin 20, Harris Shiffman,
22b, Olga Tropinina 12; Sergiy Zavgoroduy 44; iStock: 5, 6, 8, 10t, 10b, 11t, 14, 15, 18b,
26, 27, 33, 34, 36, 38, 40, 42, 43, 45; Photos.com: 9, 11b, 22t, 29, 31, 35.

All other images © Dorling Kindersley Limited
For more information see: www.dkimages.com

Discover more at
www.dk.com

Contents

DK READERS

READING
3
ALONE

Boys'Life SERIES

Let's Go
Hiking

Written by John McKinney

DK Publishing

Let's go hiking!

What do you think is America's favorite outdoor recreation? It's not cycling or soccer or swimming.

Surprise! It's hiking! Most people who hike got started when they were kids.

Hiking is taking a walk on a trail in nature. Walking to school is not hiking, and neither is walking around the mall. But walking in the forest or mountains is hiking. So is walking a path in the desert or along the seashore. Every hike is a walk but not every walk is a hike.

Hiking takes you to beautiful places you can only reach on foot. It's a great way to spend time with your friends. Trails lead to waterfalls, meadows full of wildflowers, mountaintops, swimming holes, picnic areas, and campgrounds.

You can hike with a school group, scout troop, friends, family, or park rangers and guides. It feels good to be out in the fresh air, get some exercise, and enjoy the wonders of nature.

A hike can be as short as a half-hour or a half-day, or many days long. Some people hike the same trails near home over and over again. Others explore new trails in faraway mountains. Backpackers are hikers who carry enough gear to camp overnight.

So what is there to learn about hiking? You just put one foot in front of the other, right? It's so simple.

Well, actually, there is more to hiking than just walking.

This book shares the basics of hiking so that you can better enjoy this fun way to spend time outdoors. You'll learn about hiking gear and safety. Plus, you'll get some great tips on how to make the most out of your time on the trail.

Gearing up

You don't need a lot of equipment to get started hiking. The basics are a day pack, some good hiking boots, outdoor clothing, and water.

A day pack is a smaller, soft backpack. It usually includes a hip band or waist belt for support. It's okay to begin hiking with a school backpack, but if you want to be a real hiker, you need a day pack made to carry what a hiker needs. Every hiker needs to carry basic items, such as extra clothing, food, water, and a camera.

A good day pack has padded shoulder straps, plenty of pockets, strong buckles and straps, and covered zippers. Before you buy a pack, put a little weight in it and walk around the store. Be sure the pack fits and feels comfortable.

When packing a day pack, place stuff you'll most likely use on the hike in easy to reach places. Also, put the heaviest items at the bottom of the pack and the lightest ones toward the top.

Some types of day packs can be worn around the waist.

The Ten Essentials

This list of hiking's "Ten Essentials" list was first shared among hikers in the 1930s and is still used today. Any kids who are going hiking should always check with an adult before hiking. In fact, you should always hike with an adult.

1. **Water:** Bring plenty of it and drink it before you're thirsty.

2. **Map:** Use one that shows all the trails in the area.

3. **Compass:** Goes hand-in-hand with the map. (You can bring a GPS unit, too.)

4. **Extra food:** Bring more than you think you might eat. Be prepared with energy snacks!

5. **Extra clothes:** Pack rainwear and be ready for sudden changes in weather.

6. **First Aid kit:** Include some blister treatment, too.

7. **Pocketknife:** Keep it clean and sharp.

8. **Sun protection:** Sunglasses and sunscreen.

9. **Flashlight:** You never know when you might have to hike after dark.

10. **Matches:** Waterproof matches are good to have, just in case.

More Hiking Gear Ideas:

—**Hat:** Keeps body heat in, solar heat out.

—**Camera:** Use a protective case

—**Insect repellent:** Keep those bugs away!

—**Trekking pole:** Gives you third and fourth "legs" on the trail.

—**Bandana:** Soak in water and wrap around your neck to keep you cool on the trail. Plus, hikers will find hundreds of other uses for this handy item!

Along with a day pack, you'll need good shoes, called hiking boots. Kids' lightweight boots are like sneakers with a heavier sole. Make sure they fit with plenty of toe room for downhill hiking, and are wide enough for comfort.

Synthetic socks made especially for hiking prevent blisters, stay drier, and are better than cotton ones. Take an extra pair. If you get your feet wet, you'll be happy to have dry socks to wear.

As for clothing, the word is "layering." Layering is just what it sounds like: you wear several thin layers of clothing. You can take some off if it's hot, or easily add more if it gets chilly.

A good choice when layering is a fleece jacket, which looks great and keeps you warm. It doesn't weigh much, so that when you take it off and stuff it in your pack, it's easy to carry.

Long pants are best in cold weather. Some hikers wear them in warm weather, too, because they protect against scratches, insects, and sunburn.

Many kids like to wear what they call convertible pants. These are long pants that have zippers above the knee so you can zip off the bottom half, changing them into shorts.

For eating on the trail, it's fine to pack a basic lunch with sandwich, fruit, and a cookie. However, experienced hikers like to pack a variety of healthy and high-powered trail foods that can be eaten throughout the day. Here are some ideas.

Favorite Trail Foods

Dried fruit Easy to pack, won't spoil, very tasty.

Jerky Plenty of protein. Plus you can make like a caveman and gnaw on dried meat in the wilderness!

Cheese and crackers Hard cheeses pack better than softer ones.

Ants on a Log Fill celery stalks with

Trail mix

Trail mix, or GORP (which stands for "Good Old Raisins and Peanuts"), has been a part of hiking for a long time. It starts with raisins and peanuts, but hikers have added all kinds of stuff to it over the years. You might try adding granola, M&Ms, carob chips, dried fruit, banana chips, flaked coconut, shelled sunflower seeds, soy nuts, almonds, or cashews.

peanut butter and sprinkle with raisins.

Bars Energy bars, granola bars, protein bars, sports bars, whatever you want to call them. Keep a few in your pack. If you don't eat them that day, they can keep for the next hike.

Chocolate Tastes great at home, even better on the trail. But remember, chocolate can melt in hot weather.

All about trails

A good trail is like a good guide. A good trail will take you to interesting places and will show you the best route from one place to another. The best hiking trails don't go from point A to point B in the fastest way—they take the scenic route. A good trail switchbacks (or zigzags) up and down a mountainside rather than heading straight uphill.

The first trail-makers were wild animals, breaking brush as they traveled to and from water. Native Americans used animal trails and made new ones. More than a hundred years ago, people began building trails just for hiking. Trails don't just happen—they're designed and built. What a hiker sees on a trail is often created by a trail designer.

Trails and hikes are rated by their level of difficulty—usually Easy, Moderate, or Difficult. For example, an easy hike might be less than 5 miles (8 km) with an elevation gain of less than 700 feet (215 m) or so. (That means the trail rises in height above sea level as you walk along.) A moderate hike might be 5 to 10 miles (8–16 km) with less than a 2,000-foot (610-m) elevation gain. A difficult hike might be more than 10 miles (16 km) long.

America's trails

The United States has eight long National Scenic Trails and more than 800 National Recreation Trails. The two most famous are the Appalachian  Trail (2,172 miles/3,495 km) in the the eastern United States and the Pacific Crest Trail (2,655 miles/4,272 km) in the west. Hikers who complete one of these long trails are known as end-to-enders.

Hikers can choose among many different kinds of trails. Nature trails are short and help you learn about plants. An out-and-back trail is one you use both coming and going. Many hikers like loop trails because you circle around and see something different with every step along the way. Some trails are for hikers only, while others share space with mountain bikes or horses.

On the trail

Here are some other things to keep in mind before you set out.

First, it's important to know how fast you hike (called your pace) so you can choose the right trail. Find a pace you can keep up for a long time. You need to know your limits, but you should also challenge yourself. Adults hike two to three miles an hour. Kids hike about one to two miles an hour. Your speed will vary depending on the trail's difficulty.

When you hike, be weather-wise. Dress for whatever weather you're hiking in—and expect it to change.

Know where you're hiking. Get a basic idea of where you started the hike from and where you're going. Learn how to read a trail map.

Work as a team. Offer comfort to friends or younger family members if they're slow, tired, or don't feel well. Use kindness and encourage them with positive words. Help them by carrying some of their things in your pack, or by offering water or a snack. Think about how you would want to be treated if you felt the same way—and then do it.

Cairns on a trail

There's no whining in hiking. You know how awful it is to be around someone who whines. If you feel like whining, do something else! Have a snack, drink some water, slow down, speed up, look at the view, pretend you're an animal . . . anything, but don't whine.

Hiking is fun, but there are some important safety tips. First, always stay with your fellow hikers. Second, to keep from getting lost (and to protect the environment), stay on the trail. Pay attention to signs, mileage markers, posts, and piles of stones known as cairns or ducks.

Notice the landmarks you pass, such as unusual trees or rock formations. Stop now and then to compare your progress to the trail map.

Another way to stay on course is to look behind you once in a while. See what the land looks like from the other direction. Knowing where you came from always gives you a better feel for where you're going and prepares you for the return trip.

Trail maps

When you're hiking in an unfamiliar place, you need a map that shows the trails. Some park maps are very simple and show only the trails themselves, roads, and some features such as the visitor center and picnic areas. More detailed maps show trailheads, creeks and rivers, elevations, and distances between points.

The key to reading a map is the scale, which shows how many inches represent a mile. If one inch equals one mile on the map, and it's about three inches from the trailhead to your destination, that's a three-mile hike.

Also check the map's legend, which tells you what the symbols on the map mean. You might see symbols for a campground, rest stop, ranger's hut, or lookout point.

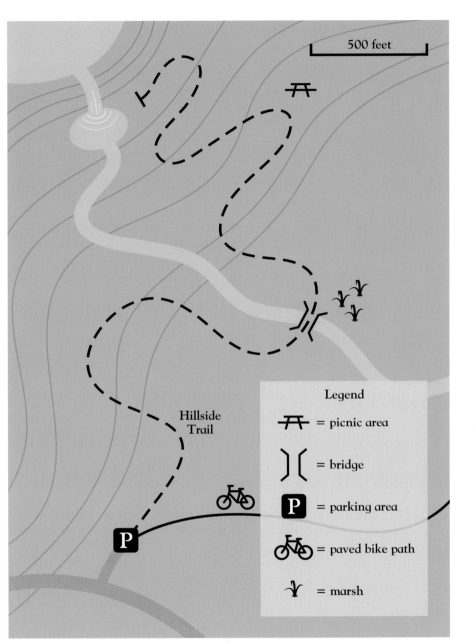

Legend

⊤⊤ = picnic area

)(= bridge

P = parking area

🚲 = paved bike path

🌱 = marsh

Hillside Trail

This simple trail map shows the path you'll walk on. You can see how long the trail is and where you can stop to rest. Elevation lines (in green) show a nearby hill.

Fun on the trail

Besides time with your friends, other things make a good hike great—like water. Swim, splash, or just cool your feet in a lake or stream.

For some hikers, the best thing about being out in nature is seeing animals and interesting plants and trees. Ask park rangers to point out places where you're likely to spot wildlife while you're on your hike.

Maybe you'll get summit fever, which sounds like something that makes you sick, but is actually a good thing for a hiker to catch. It means that you hike to the top, or summit, of mountains.

Another fun thing to do is to take lots of pictures of your hike. Start with pictures of the trailhead or trail signs. Plus, along with taking pictures of your smiling buddies, get close-ups on nature. Photo tip: One big flower shot close-up is usually a better image than a lot of flowers in a faraway meadow.

Places to hike

Any place outdoors can be a good place to hike. Let's take a look at some popular hiking environments.

Most people first think of hiking in a thick forest. A forest trail gets you close to the moss on the trunks, the lichen hanging from the limbs, and the flowering plants that grow in the shade.

Forests that have never been logged are called ancient forests, or old-growth forests. They are very special places to hike. Imagine 400-year old maple, hemlock, or birch or 2,000-year old redwoods—among the world's tallest trees.

It's hard to keep your sense of direction when you're surrounded by trees. To help stay on the trail, look for trail markers such as colored disks or paint blazes on trees.

Fall is a great time to be in the woods when the leaves change color to red, orange, yellow, and gold. Of course, evergreen forests stay green all year around— except when they're covered with snow.

The desert has a beauty all its own. Some of America's largest and most awesome national parks—Death Valley and Grand Canyon—are desert wonders. You'll see red rock peaks that touch the clouds, palm trees surrounding a hidden pool, and sand dunes higher than a 30-story building.

Desert hiking trails are rarely the first trails hikers think about, but the desert does have great hiking if you know where to go. Hike up a sand dune (two steps up, one step back!), make your way (carefully!) around spiky cactus and yucca, or climb a desert peak for a view that goes on forever. Be on the lookout for the desert's special creatures—the very slow desert tortoise and the very quick big-horned sheep.

Be sure to do your desert hike in the cooler parts of the day—morning and late afternoon. Wear sun protection and a hat, and drink lots and lots of water.

For some hikers, a hike is not a hike unless it reaches a mountain top. It feels great to stand on top of a peak, look down at the world below, and realize how far you climbed. Some hikers like to climb every peak in a mountain range or take a dozen different trails to the top of one favorite mountain.

As you climb higher up a mountain the views get better. With changes in elevation come changes in the natural world: from bushes to trees, from trees to meadows, and from meadows to the rocky top of the mountain. When you hike above the tree line (or timber line) the views get really terrific.

The higher you climb the colder and windier it gets. Remember to take warm clothes. Above 5,000 to 6,000 feet (1,500 to 1,800 m), you'll notice the air gets thinner. You'll need to slow down.

The coast or seashore can be a great place to hike. Walk across white sand beaches, along tall bluffs, across islands, or through coastal forests. Sometimes you can hike a mile or two away from a popular beach and discover a whole new world—or at least a great place to fish or surf.

Observe—but don't disturb— the starfish, hermit crabs, and other life in tidepools. Hike to a lighthouse and take in the view. Check out the many shore birds and look out to sea for seals diving, dolphins jumping, or even whales spouting.

The time to go beach hiking, tidepool exploring, or seashell collecting is at low tide. Check a tide chart and plan your day so that you begin hiking a few hours before low tide and finish a few hours after.

Backpacking

Backpacking is a combination of hiking and camping. A backpacker hikes into the backcountry to spend one night or more there. Backpackers carry supplies and gear for preparing meals and sleeping.

Backpackers can travel into wilderness areas farther from people and cities than day hikers. Many backpacking trips take place over a weekend while others are a week or many weeks in length.

Backpackers take the Ten Essentials and the gear carried by day hikers. They also take a tent, sleeping bag, and cookware. Carrying your bedroom and kitchen on your back can be heavy. Backpacker's Rule No. 1: If you want it, you have to carry it! Backpackers look for lightweight gear. A four-pound (1.8-kg) tent is way better than an eight-pound (3.6-kg) tent!

Backpackers often use small liquid-fuel camp stoves. They use the stoves to boil water to add to freeze-dried backpacking food. Some of these instant meals are yummy and some are, well . . . not so yummy! Make sure to taste-test them before you hit the trail! Of course, nothing tastes too bad when you're really hungry and camping in a beautiful place.

Don't expect restrooms, hot

showers, and a camp store when you backpack into a trail camp.
A hike-in camp might have just

a table and a fire ring. Some trail camps are just small patches of level ground.

The best way to learn about backpacking is to go on an overnight hike with an experienced backpacker. Planning ahead to make sure you have a safe route and all your gear is the best way to make sure you have fun.

A hiking trip

Now that you've read about the basic rules of hiking, let's take a hike!

Imagine a loop trail that takes you and your friends through a forest to the top of a hill. It returns along a stream.

You'll pack the Ten Essentials, of course. Don't forget some trail mix. You have a good trail map and tips from the park ranger. You should get an early start because it gets very warm on the mountain by midday. Watch out for a bad length of trail on the return loop, and check out the waterfall!

The weather report calls for "mostly sunny with a chance of showers." Be smart and pack your rainwear!

The sign at the trailhead reads 2.5 miles (4 km) to the peak. Let's go!

At first, your group travels through the forest. The birds are singing and it's easy hiking. Then the trail climbs out of the trees and gets very steep. Goodbye shade, hello hot slopes. You zip off the legs of your pants and turn them into hiking shorts. It's hard walking uphill, even though you're on a well-built trail.

One of your friends is new to hiking and is having trouble keeping up. Stop

for a drink of water, give him some trail mix (with chocolate!) and tell him, "You can do it!" You put him in the front of the line and all of sudden he turns into a rocket ship and blasts up the hill!

Before you know it, you're all standing at the top of the mountain.

What a view! Mountains and more mountains. And lots of blue sky, so you're not going to need your rainwear.

Hike down the mountain to a meadow where a deer and a fawn leap across the trail. As the deer look back at you, be quick with the camera and take some great pictures of the deer standing in some wildflowers.

Near a stream you reach a trail
junction without a sign. You know to
take a left and hike downstream back
to the trailhead. But after a few minutes
you realize you're not going in the
direction of the waterfall. You check
the map. Oops—should have gone right
back there instead of left.

You double back and soon reach the waterfall, which isn't very big, but big enough to fill a waist-high pool. Time for a quick dip to cool off!

As you head downhill to finish up your hike, you remember the great pictures you took, with your mind *and* your camera—the kid new to hiking looking sad then happy . . . another kid with a face half-covered in dirt and half in chocolate . . . everyone standing proudly on the top of the mountain.

Those pictures—and your memories—will be great to share with family and friends—until you start planning your next hiking adventure!

Find out more

Books

The Complete Walker IV
By Colin Fletcher
You'll need a big backpack to carry this 800-page book.
But if you find it in a library, you can discover tons of
useful hiking information. This is the latest edition of
a book that hikers have been using for more than 40
years.

Hike
By John McKinney
The author of *Let's Go Hiking!* has written other
books, including this one, which offers more in-depth
tips about hiking, including gear, routes, and even
recipes for trail mix!

Hiking
By Adam Klein
Another close-up look at hiking, including some other
ideas on places you can hike.

Tail of the Scorpion: Adventure with the Parkers
By Mike Graf
This novel is part of a series that follows the adventures
of James and Morgan and their parents. The family
visits famous National Parks and other outdoor areas
and enjoys adventurous hikes.

Web sites

American Hiking Society
www.AmericanHiking.org
Find a local hiking club and learn more about trails, hiking and National Trails Day.

Boy's Life Magazine
www.boyslife.org
On our official Web site, you can find excellent advice about hiking and other outdoor activities.

The Trailmaster
www.TheTrailmaster.com
Organized by the author of *Let's Go Hiking!,* this site includes hiking tips, trails, and tales.

Note to Parents: These Web sites are not endorsed by Boy Scouts of America or DK Publishing and have not been completely examined. However, at press time, they provided the sort of information described. Internet experts always suggest that you work with your children to help them understand how to safely navigate the Web.

Glossary

Backcountry
Areas of land beyond where roads reach, often heavily forested.

Blazes
Marks on trees, poles, or elsewhere that mark a trail.

Bluff
A low cliff with a flat front, usually next to water.

Cairns
Piles of stones that mark the trail. Also called "ducks."

Day pack
Small, soft backpack made especially for hikers.

Degree of difficulty
Measurement of how hard the hike is. Ratings include easy, moderate, difficult.

End-to-enders
Hikers who walk the entire length of very long marked trails.

Elevation
Measurement of altitude above sea level. The difficulty of a hike goes along with how much elevation gain is required.

Freeze-dried
Has water removed by a special process. Adding water back in makes freeze-dried food edible.

Grade
The amount of elevation change (steepness) between two points on the trail.

GORP
Abbreviation for "Good Old Raisins & Peanuts," another term for trail mix.

Junction
The point at which a path or trail meets another path or trail.

Layering
Wearing several thin layers of outdoor clothing rather than one heavy one.

Lichen
A plant that grows on top of other plants or rocks.

Logged
Cut-down trees.

Loop trail
A trail that completes a circle.

Moderate
Between easy and difficult.

Nature trail
A path with signs identifying plants and describing other natural features.

Pace
The speed at which you walk or hike.

Summit
The top of a mountain.

Switchback
A zigzag, back-and-forth route up a mountain.

Synthetic
Manmade, not natural.

Terrain
The natural features of the land.

Timber line
The place on a mountain above which trees don't grow.

Trailhead
Start of the trail.